How many animals did Moses take on the ark?

Moses didn't take anything on the ark. Noah did!

What animals were the last to leave the ark?

Elephants. They had to pack their trunks.

What animals didn't come on the ark in pairs?

Worms. They came in apples.

Knock-Knock.

Who's there?

Noah.

Noah who?

Noah good knock-knock joke?

What's black and white and green?

A seasick zebra.

What's black and white and blue all over?

A skunk at the North Pole.

What is black and white and lives in Hawaii?

A lost penguin.

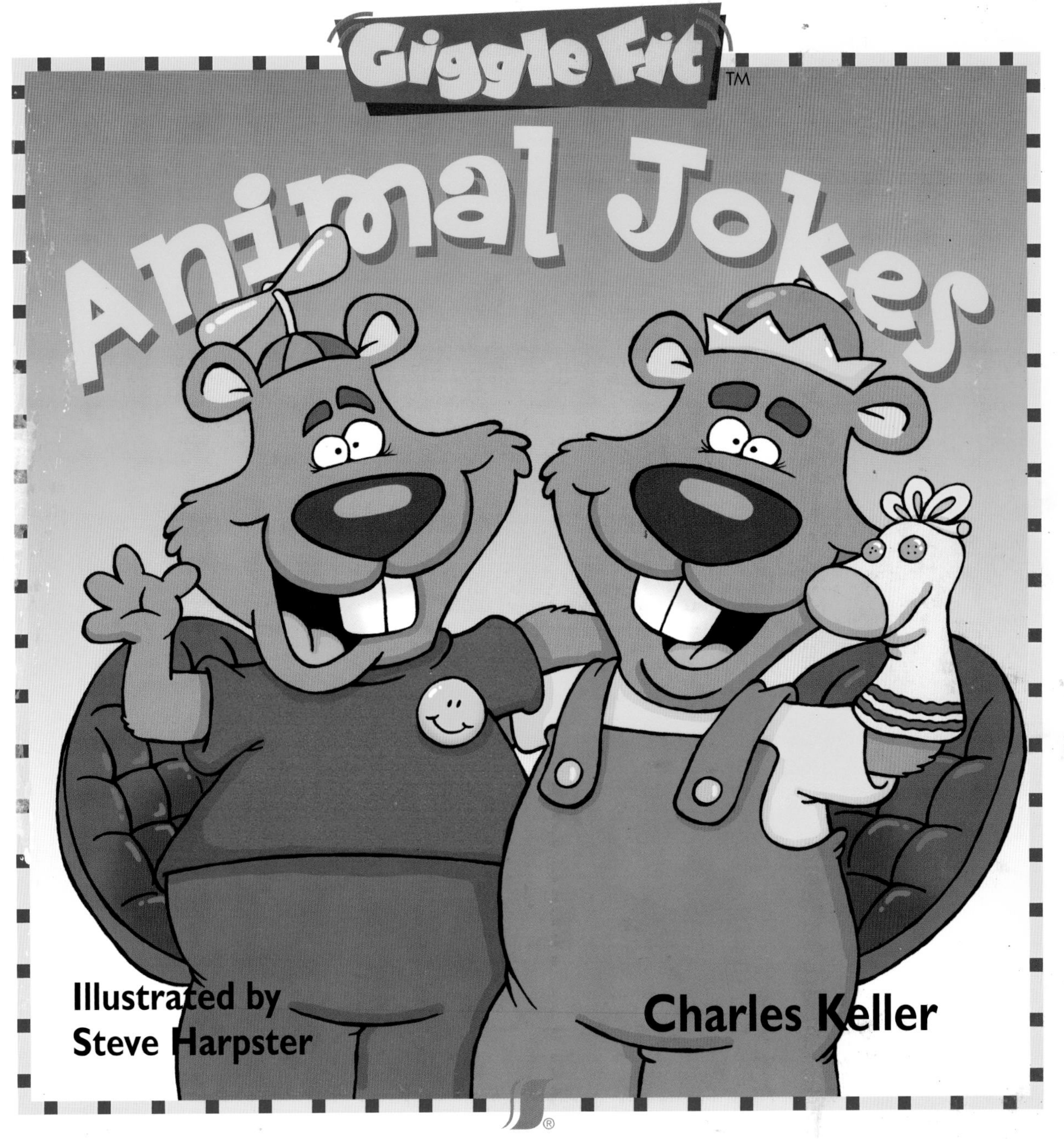

Sterling Publishing Co., Inc.
New York

Library of Congress Cataloging-in-Publication Data Available

10 9 8 7 6 5 4 3 2 1

Published in paperback 2004 by Sterling Publishing Co., Inc.
387 Park Avenue South, New York, N.Y. 10016

Distributed in Canada by Sterling Publishing
c/o Canadian Manda Group, One Atlantic Avenue, Suite 105
Toronto, Ontario, Canada M6K 3E7
Distributed in Great Britain by Chris Lloyd at Orca
Book Services, Stanley House, Fleets Lane, Poole BH15 3AJ, England
Distributed in Australia by Capricorn Link (Australia) Pty. Ltd.
P.O. Box 704, Windsor, NSW 2756 Australia

Printed in China

Sterling ISBN 1-4027-0438-0 Hardcover
ISBN 1-4027-1760-1 Paperback

What has to crawl 12 times to go a foot?

An inchworm.

Why did the worm oversleep?

Because it didn't want to get caught by the early bird.

What's the best way to get rid of a 100-pound worm in your garden?

Get a 1,000-pound robin.

What insect breathes fire?
A dragonfly.

What insect can't say yes or no?
A may-bee.

How do fleas travel?
They itchhike.

What's green and goes, "Clomp, clomp, clomp, clomp, clomp, clomp"?
A grasshopper trying out his new hiking boots.

What would you get if you crossed a praying mantis and a termite?
An insect that says grace before eating your house.

Where do bugs buy their groceries?
At the flea market.

What has fifty legs but can't walk?
Half a centipede.

What would you get if you crossed a centipede and a parrot?
A walkie-talkie.

Why don't centipedes play football?
By the time they get their shoes on, the game is over.

What do bees say to each other when they come home?
"Hi, honey!"

What did the bee say to the flower?
"Hey, bud, what time do you open?"

How do stinging insects talk to each other on a computer?
They use bee-mail.

How did the bee get to school?
It took a buzz.

Why did the bee go to the doctor?

It had hives.

What is a bee with a low buzz?

A mumble bee.

What is a bee's favorite country?

Stingapore.

Knock-Knock.

Who's there?

Honeybee.

Honeybee who?

Honeybee nice and open the door.

Knock-Knock.
Who's there?
Owl goes.
Owl goes who?
Yes, I know it does.

What do birds eat for dessert?
Chocolate chirp cookies.

Why do birds fly south for the winter?
They don't want to wait for the bus.

Who do birds marry?
Their tweethearts.

What birds hang out around the ski slopes?

Skigulls.

What do you call a bird in winter?

A brrrd.

Why was the little bird punished at school?

It was caught peeping during a test.

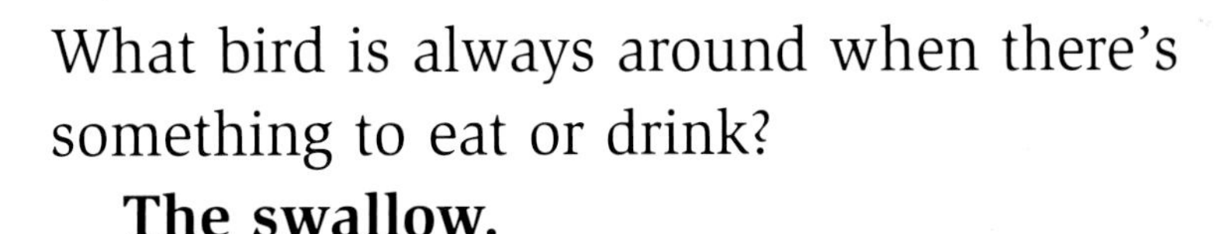

What bird is always around when there's something to eat or drink?

The swallow.

What size T-shirt should you buy for a 200-pound egg?

Eggs-tra large.

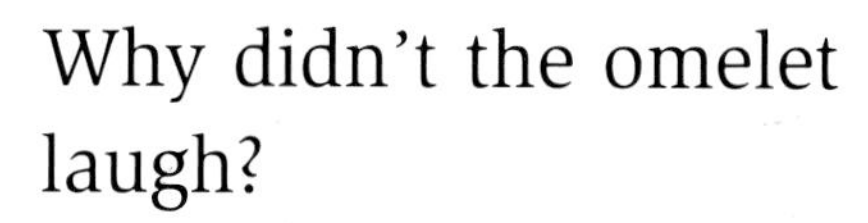

Why didn't the omelet laugh?

It didn't get the yolk.

What would you get if you crossed an earthquake and a chicken?

Scrambled eggs.

What would you get if you crossed a chicken and a guitar?

A chicken that plucks itself.

Why did the chicken cross the road twice?
Because she was a double-crosser.

What did the chicken say when she laid a square egg?
"Ouch!"

Why did the hen go to the doctor?
To get a chick-up.

Why was the chicken sick?
It had people pox.

What bird hunt is never successful?

A wild goose chase.

Why do people get goose bumps?

Because camel bumps are too big.

Why did the goose cross the road?

To get a gander at the other side.

What would you get if you crossed a goose and a rhinoceros?

An animal that honks before it runs you over.

Who stole the soap?
The robber ducky.

What is a duck's favorite snack?
Quacker jacks.

If a duck says, "Quack, quack," when it walks, what does it say when it runs?
"Quick, quick!"

What did the lady duck say to the sales clerk when she bought a lipstick?
"Please put it on my bill."

What two dogs are opposites?
Hot dogs and chili dogs.

How does a hot dog wear its hair?
In a bun.

What do you call the top of a dog house?
The woof.

Does your dog bite strangers?
Only when he doesn't know them.

How do you cure fleas on a dog?
It all depends on what's wrong with the fleas.

Why do dogs make better pets than elephants?
Elephants keep getting stuck in the front door.

Why do fire trucks have dogs on them?
To find the fire hydrant.

Is your dog paper-trained?
No, he can't read a thing.

If dogs go to obedience school, where do cats go?
Kittygarten.

What magazine do cats like to read?
Good Mousekeeping.

Knock-Knock.
Who's there?
Lettie.
Lettie who?
Lettie cat out of the bag.

What cat likes to go bowling?
An alley cat.

If there were ten cats in a boat and one jumped out, how many would be left?

None, because they were all copycats.

Where do cats go to dance?

To the fur ball.

What cat lives in the ocean?

An octopus.

Why wouldn't they let the cat use the computer?

She kept chasing the mouse.

When does a mouse weigh as much as an elephant?
When the scale is broken.

What's the difference between mice and rice?
You can't throw mice at weddings.

When is it bad luck to have a black cat follow you?
When you're a mouse.

Knock-Knock.
Who's there?
Flea.
Flea who?
Flea blind mice.

Where do frogs sit?
On toadstools.

What is a frog's favorite flower?
A crocus.

How did the frog win the jumping race?
By leaps and bounds.

What is a frog's favorite soft drink?
Croak-a-cola.

Why does a turtle live in a shell?

Because it can't afford an apartment.

Why is it great to be a turtle?

You never have far to walk home.

Where does a turtle go out to eat?

In a slow-food restaurant.

What do you say to speed up a turtle?

"Make it snappy."

What do you call a rabbit that is owned by a beetle?
A bug's bunny.

What is the opposite of the Easter bunny?
The Wester bunny.

Where do rabbits go
to hear people sing?
To the hopera.

Where do you find
flying rabbits?
In the hare force.

What would you get if you crossed a robot and a skunk?

R 2 PU.

What is the most famous skunk statue in Egypt?

The Stinx.

If a skunk wrote a popular book, what list would it be on?

The best smeller list.

What would you get if you crossed a skunk with a fairy?

Stinkerbell.

How did the sick sheep get to the hospital?
By lambulance.

Dogs have fleas. What do sheep have?
Fleece.

Knock-Knock.
Who's there?
Babar.
Babar who?
Babar black sheep.

Why didn't the lamb make a sound all day?
It didn't like to bleat between meals.

What gives milk and has two wheels?

A cow on a motorcycle.

What would you get if you crossed a kangaroo with a cow?

A kangamoo.

Why did the cow cross the road?

To get to the udder side.

What do cows read in the morning?

The moos-paper.

What cheese does a cow like?
Moo-zarella.

What did the mama cow say to the baby cow?
It's pasture bedtime.

Knock-Knock.
Who's there?
Cows.
Cows who?
No — cows moo.

What do cows say
when they cry?
"Moo-hoo!"

Why didn't the horse draw the cart?

He couldn't hold a pencil.

What did the horse say after it finished its hay?

"That was the last straw."

Why did the horse put on the blanket?

He was a little colt.

Why aren't horses well dressed?

They wear shoes but no socks.

What kind of vehicle does a hog drive?
A pig-up truck.

What number does a pig call in an emergency?
Swine-one-one.

What's a pig's favorite fairy tale?
Slopping beauty.

What position does a pig play in baseball?
Short slop.

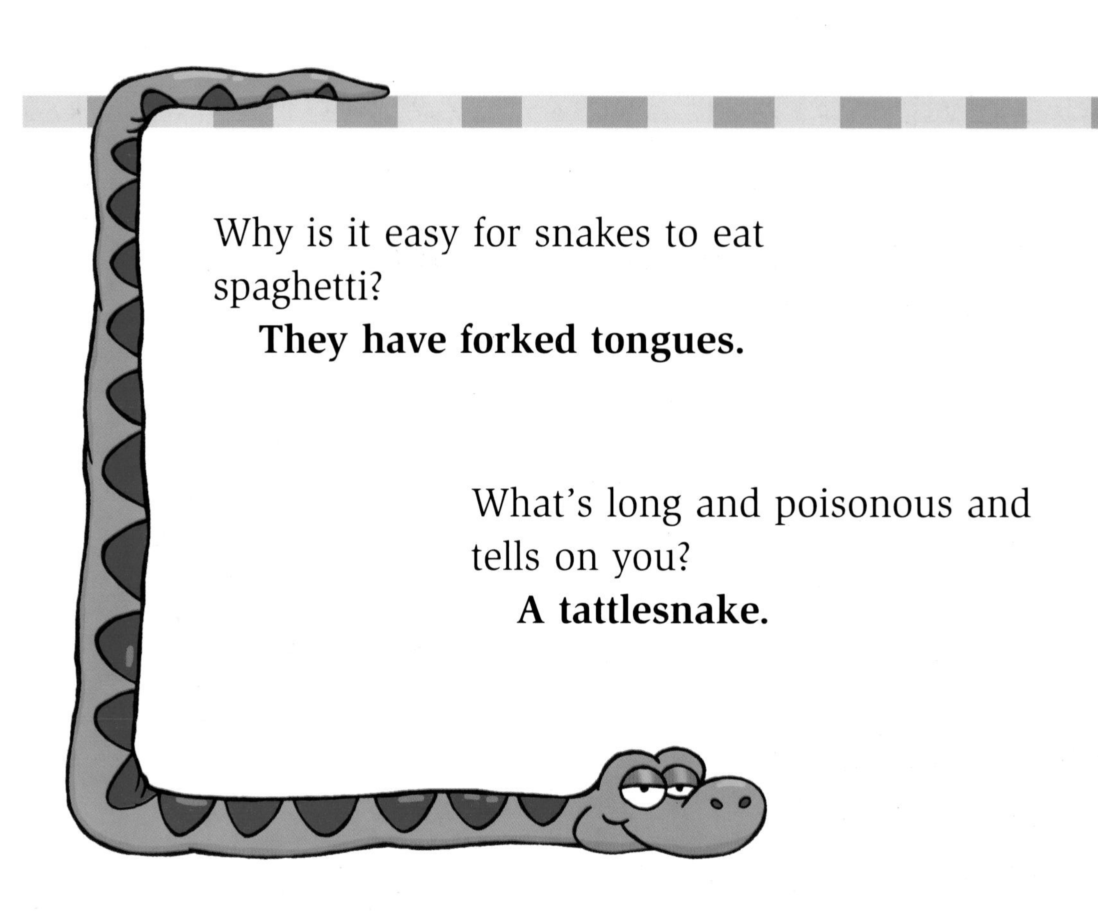

Why is it easy for snakes to eat spaghetti?
They have forked tongues.

What's long and poisonous and tells on you?
A tattlesnake.

How do snakes sign their letters?
Love and hisses.

Why do they measure snakes in inches?
Because they have no feet.

What is long and thin and goes "Hith, Hith"?
A snake with a lisp.

Why did the baby snake cry?
It lost its rattle.

Why is it so hard to play a joke on a snake?
You can't pull its leg.

Knock-Knock.
Who's there?
Snake.
Snake who?
"Snake me out to the ball game..."

What's the difference between a dog and a marine scientist?

One wags a tail, the other tags a whale.

Who watches little squids?

Babysquidders.

What sea creature can add?

An octo-plus.

What is the hardest thing about being an octopus?
Washing your hands before dinner.

What goes, "Clomp, clomp, clomp, clomp, clomp, clomp, clomp, squish"?
An octopus with one shoe off.

What do whales chew?
Blubber gum.

What do clams and oysters do over the holidays?
Shellebrate.

Who grants the wishes of fishes?

Their fairy codmother.

What's the difference between a fish and a piano?

You can't tune a fish.

What do you call a fish without an eye?

A fsh.

Why don't fish play tennis?

They don't want to get caught in the net.

Why did the otter cross the road?
To get to the otter side.

Where do otters come from?
Otter space.

Knock-Knock.
Who's there?
Otter.
Otter who?
Otter apologize for some of these jokes.

What snack do little monkeys have with their milk?
Chocolate chimp cookies.

What monkey can fly?
A hot air baboon.

What language do chimpanzees speak?
Chimpanese.

What did the monkey say to the vine?
"Thanks for letting me hang around."

What did the leopard say in the cafeteria?
"Save me a spot."

How do bears like campers?
Raw.

Why do leopards have spotted coats?
Because the tigers bought all the striped ones.

What would you get if you crossed a tiger with a Japanese restaurant?
Man-eating sushi.

Knock-Knock.
Who's there?
Lionel.
Lionel who?
Lionel roar if you don't feed it.

What weighs 2,000 pounds and is covered with lettuce and special sauce?

A big MacElephant.

Why do elephants have wrinkled ankles?

They tie their sneakers too tight.

Why don't elephants tip bellhops?

They like to carry their own trunks.

Why do elephants have trunks?

Because they can't fit all their stuff in their makeup case.

Why are elephant rides cheaper than pony rides?

Because elephants work for peanuts.

What elephant flies?

A Dumbo jet.

How can you tell that an elephant is living in your house?

By the enormous pajamas in your closet.

How can you tell if an elephant is in your cereal box?

Read the label.

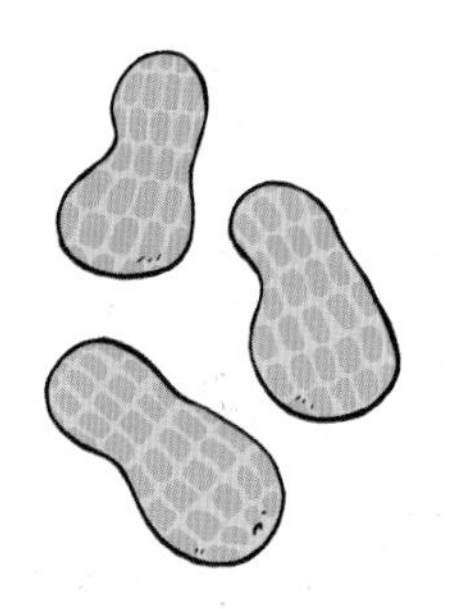

Why do bears have fur?
So their underwear won't show.

What bear loves to wash her hair?
Winnie the Shampoo.

What's a polar bear's favorite cereal?
Ice Krispies.

Why does a mink have fur?
If it didn't, it would be a little bear.

What would you get if you crossed a greyhound with a giraffe?

A dog that chases airplanes.

Can giraffes have babies?

No, they can only have giraffes.

What is worse than a giraffe with a sore throat?

An octopus with tennis elbow.

Does a giraffe get a sore throat if it gets wet feet?

Yes, but not until the following week.

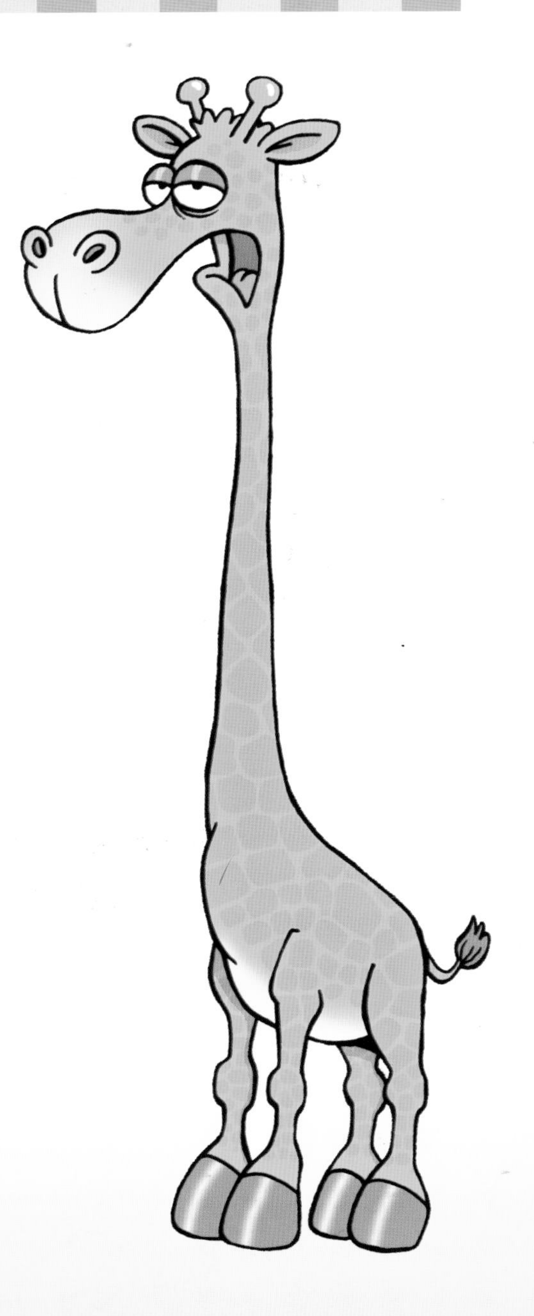

What would you get if you crossed a kangaroo and a crocodile?

Leaping lizards.

What newspaper do reptiles read?

The Scaly News.

What is a sick crocodile?

An illigator.

What does an alligator sing?

Scales.

What is it called when two spiders get married?
A webbing.

On what day do spiders have a good meal?
Flyday.

What do spiders eat with their hamburgers?
French flies.

SPIDER: Will you share your curds with me?
MISS MUFFET: No whey.

How does one amoeba speak to another amoeba?

On a cell phone.

What do you call a whale that talks too much?

A blubbermouth.

What would you get if you crossed a parrot and a caterpillar?

A chatterpillar.

Knock-Knock.

Who's there?

Hyena.

Hyena who?

Hyena tree sat a parrot.

What jungle animal is always complaining?

A whinoceros.

What is a llama's favorite vegetable?
Llama beans.

Knock-Knock.
Who's there?
Moose.
Moose who?
Moose be love.

Knock-Knock.
Who's there?
Llama.
Llama who?
Llama Yankee Doodle Dandy.

What animal puts other creatures into a trance?
A hypnopotamus.

What's gray on the inside and brown on the outside?
A chocolate-covered dinosaur.

What would you get if you crossed Bambi with a ghost?
Bamboo.

What's the best way to see a monster?
From half a mile away.

What's large, yellow, and lives in Scotland?
The Loch Ness canary.

Knock-Knock.

Who's there?

Zookeeper.

Zookeeper who?

Zookeeper your shirt on!

Knock-Knock.

Who's there?

Safari.

Safari who?

Safari so good.

Knock-Knock.

Who's there?

Weevil.

Weevil who?

Weevil meet again.

INDEX